The Tiny Book of Lawyer Jokes

The Tiny Book of Lawyer Jokes

Edward Phillips

Illustrated by
Tony Blundell

HarperCollins*Publishers*

HarperCollins*Publishers*
77–85 Fulham Palace Road,
Hammersmith, London W6 8JB

www.**fire**and**water**.com

This paperback edition 2001
1 3 5 7 9 8 6 4 2

Previously published in Great Britain
by Angus & Robertson (UK) 1991

ISBN 0 00 712877 0

Set in Stone Sans by Rowland Phototypesetting Ltd,
Bury St Edmunds, Suffolk
Printed and bound in Great Britain by Scotprint, Haddington

A lawyer had just won a case on behalf of a client who had sued his employers for negligence after falling down a disused lift shaft. When the client was presented with the bill, he was furious.

'You've taken over two-thirds of my damages!' he stormed. 'How do you justify that?'

'Because,' said the lawyer, 'I provided the skill, the knowledge and the legal expertise to win the case.'

'But I provided the case itself,' protested the client.

'Oh, that,' scoffed the lawyer. 'Anybody can fall down a lift shaft.'

In a case of estrangement, a lawyer acting for the wife asked his client to come and see him in his office.

'Well, Mrs Robinson,' he said, 'I have finally arrived at a settlement with your husband which I feel is eminently fair to both of you.'

'Fair to both of us!' said the wife indignantly. 'I could have done that myself! Why do you think I hired a lawyer?'

The barrister had risen to dazzling heights of eloquence in defence of his client. 'One moment, Mr Kenwood,' interrupted the judge. 'I don't quite understand. You are protesting your client's innocence but he has already pleaded guilty.'

'I know that, my lord,' declared the barrister, 'but you and I know better than to believe a single word a man with his criminal record has to say.'

'Do you have a criminal lawyer in this town?'
   'Well, we're pretty sure we do but we haven't been able to prove it yet.'

Irish defence counsel in a paternity suit: 'And in conclusion, my client emphatically denies that he is the father of the twins – or, indeed, of either one of them.'

Lawyer: An individual whose principal role is to protect his clients from others of his profession.

Anonymous

A lawyer was showing a friend around his garden of which he was justly proud. The friend noticed that the herbaceous borders were almost entirely filled with the pretty little plant known as honesty. 'I thought you'd be impressed,' said the lawyer. 'There's an old saying that honesty won't grow in a lawyer's garden. I think this completely disproves the saying!'

'On the other hand,' remarked the friend with a smile, 'it might just prove that you're no lawyer!'

After a very lengthy and tedious cross-examination, a lawyer suddenly broke off and protested to the judge, 'Your Honour, one of the jurors is asleep!'

'Well, you put him to sleep,' replied the judge, 'you wake him up!'

Irish barrister: 'It has been established that the offence was committed at half past twelve at night on the morning of the following day.'

A young lawyer joined his father's firm and the old man decided to turn over part of his practice to his son. A few weeks later, the young man burst into his father's office, full of smiles and said, 'Guess what! I've just settled that Macmillan case that we've been working on for the last twenty years!'

'You've done what?' exclaimed the father. 'You idiot! I gave you that case as an annuity!'

A lawyer's wife became fed up with her brilliant husband who always seemed so sure of himself on points of law. One afternoon, when their grandfather clock had just struck one she said, 'If I were to smash that clock to pieces with a hammer, could I be charged with killing time?'

'Oh, no,' said her husband. 'It would be a case of self-defence – the clock struck first.'

A rich businessman was involved in a lawsuit which dragged on and on for years. Finally he went round to see his lawyer and said, 'Look here, this thing has gone on too long. I'm tired of the whole business and I want to settle.'

'Settle!' cried the lawyer. 'Oh, no! I'm determined to fight this case down to your last penny!'

A woman was suing her neighbour for slander and defamation of character. Under cross-examination, her counsel asked her to tell the court exactly what words the neighbour had used. 'Oh, I couldn't do that, sir,' protested the woman. 'The things she said weren't fit for any decent person to hear.'

'All right,' said counsel. 'Just come over here and whisper them to the judge.'

A man who had been hurt in a motor accident spent several weeks in hospital. After his release, he was hobbling along the street on crutches when he met an old friend. 'Hello, Jim!' said the friend. 'Glad to see you up and about again. How long will it be before you can get rid of those crutches?'

'Well,' said Jim, 'my doctor says I can get along without them now, but my lawyer says I can't.'

Counsel for the defence was being particularly scathing. 'Now you claim,' he said to the plaintiff, 'that you were struck by a Range Rover, but your evidence is very confused and muddled. Are you sure it was a Range Rover or something resembling a Range Rover?'

'It resembled one all right,' said the plaintiff grimly. 'In fact, I was forcibly struck by the resemblance.'

In a case in a Dublin court, defence counsel claimed that the accused was not drunk but merely in a state of great excitement. In support he called the accused's doctor to the witness stand and asked him, 'Is it not true that the accused has a very excitable nature – have you, in fact, seen him on other occasions when he was highly excited?'

'Oh, indeed I have,' replied the doctor, 'frequently – even when sober.'

A man accused of fraud approached his counsel during a recess and demanded that another lawyer be provided to work with him. 'But why?' asked the barrister. 'Aren't you satisfied with the way I'm handling the case?'

'Yes,' said the accused. 'But the other side's got two lawyers. When one of them is talking, the other's sitting there and thinking. When you're talking, there isn't anyone doing any thinking.'

A farm labourer accused of stealing a wheelbarrow protested his innocence in court. In examination, prosecuting counsel said, 'You say you are innocent, yet you have heard the evidence of two witnesses who swear that they saw you take the wheelbarrow.'

'That's nothing,' scoffed the accused. 'I can produce a dozen witnesses who will swear that they didn't see me take it.'

A tradesman who was unable to obtain payment of a bill consulted a lawyer. 'Now you say this man owes you a considerable sum,' said the lawyer. 'What did he say when you presented your bill?'

'He told me to go to the devil,' replied the tradesman. 'And so I came round to you.'

Lawyer: One skilled in circumvention of the law.

Ambrose Bierce

A woman visited her family solicitor and said, 'I'd like to go over my will again, Mr Jenks. I'm a bit worried about . . .'

'Don't you worry about a thing, Mrs Smith,' said the solicitor, 'just leave it all to me.'

'I suppose I might as well,' said Mrs Smith with a sigh. 'You'll get it all in the end.'

A well-known lawyer commissioned a portrait in oils and was very pleased with the result. The painting showed him in a casual pose with one hand in his pocket. A friend remarked that it would have been much more realistic if it had showed him with his hand in someone else's pocket.

It has been said that Moses was a great lawgiver but the fact that he limited himself to only ten commandments and kept them short and easy to understand shows that he was no lawyer.

An elderly and very learned judge ruled against a young barrister on a point of law. The young lawyer so far forgot himself as to say loudly, 'My lord, I am amazed!' His leader, a senior barrister, hurriedly rose to his feet. 'My lord, I must apologise for my young friend's hasty and unconsidered remark. When he is as old as I am, he will not be amazed at anything your lordship says.'

'You seem to be in some distress,' said the kindly judge to the witness. 'Is anything the matter?'

'Well, your Honour,' said the witness, 'I swore to tell the truth and nothing but the truth, but every time I try, some lawyer objects.'

Counsel: 'Now were you or were you not bitten on the premises?'

Witness: 'Well, anatomy's not my strong point, sir, but I'll tell you this – I couldn't sit down for a week!'

At an important trial, a judge consistently ignored plaintiff's counsel. Despite the barrister's continued protests that he represented the plaintiff, the judge took no notice other than to instruct counsel to sit down. At last, counsel could stand it no longer. He jumped to his feet and shouted, 'My lord, *I* represent the plaintiff and I am trying to do the best I can for my client.'

'Exactly,' said the judge. 'That's why I keep telling you to sit down.'

A very successful and elderly barrister was sitting at the breakfast table reading the *Law Review*. His wife sat opposite him in silence, just as she had done every morning for the last thirty years. Thinking to break the boredom, she suddenly said, 'Anything interesting in the *Law Review* this morning, dear?'

Without looking up, the barrister grunted, 'Don't be silly, dear.'

An old juryman was being sworn in. 'Speak up!' he said to the clerk of the court. 'I can't hear what you're saying.'

'Are you deaf?' asked the judge.

'Yes, my lord – I'm deaf in one ear.'

Counsel for the defence jumped to his feet. 'My lord, I request that this man be excused. It is essential that jurymen should hear both sides.'

First lawyer: 'My lord, despite the fact that my learned friend for the defence is an unmitigated scoundrel . . .'

Second lawyer: 'My lord, we all know that my learned friend for the prosecution is a notorious liar . . .'

Judge: 'Counsel will kindly confine their remarks to such matters as are in dispute.'

A lawyer was called to account by his colleagues for taking less than the usual fee from a client, thus undercutting their normal charges. When he explained that he had taken all that the man had, he was honourably acquitted.

At a cocktail party, a lawyer was trying to obtain some free medical advice from a doctor. 'Tell me, doctor,' he said, 'which side is it best to lie on?'

'The side that pays you the biggest retainer,' replied the doctor.

Two men were walking through a cemetery. They stopped before a tombstone which bore the following inscription: 'Here lies a lawyer and an honest man.' One turned to the other and said, 'You wouldn't think there'd be room for two men in such a small grave.'

Irish barrister: 'Were you in the vicinity of the accused when he committed the crime?'
Irish witness: 'No, sir – but I was standing next to him.'

Barrister addressing the jury: 'The only failing which the prisoner has is that of relying on thieves and rogues of the worst kind. Gentlemen of the jury, the unhappy man in the dock puts implicit faith in you.'

The widow was in a complaining mood. 'Don't talk to me about lawyers!' she confided to a friend. 'I've had so much trouble settling my late husband's estate, sometimes I wish he'd never died!'

A lawyer was talking to a man who had served as a juror on a number of occasions. 'Tell me,' he said, 'who has the most influence on you in court – the lawyers, the Judge or the witnesses?'

'Well,' said the experienced juryman, 'I'm a plain man and I'm not influenced by the lawyers or the judge or the witnesses. I just look at the man in the dock and I say to myself, "If he's not done nothing, why is he here?" And I bring 'em all in guilty.'

A young man appeared as a witness in a court case. Prosecuting counsel was not at all happy with his evidence and said sharply, 'Has anyone been telling you what to say in court?'

'Yes, sir,' replied the young man. 'My father.'

'I see,' said the lawyer. 'And what exactly did he tell you?'

'He said the lawyers would try to get me all mixed up but if I stuck to the truth, I'd be all right.'

'I do wish you would pay a little attention to what I am saying to you,' said a barrister to an awkward witness.

'I'm already paying as little as I can,' said the witness.

Counsel for the complainant in a divorce case was examining his client on the stand. 'Now let me see if we have all the facts straight,' he said. 'You maintain that every night when you returned home from work, you discovered that your wife was hiding a different man in the wardrobe. Is that correct?'

'Yes, it is,' said the husband.

'And this, of course, was very upsetting to you.'

'Of course it was! I never had any room to hang up my clothes!'

A famous barrister died and many members of the legal fraternity attended his funeral. One of them was delayed and did not arrive until the minister was halfway through his sermon. As he took his seat, he whispered to his neighbour, 'Have I missed much?'

'No,' his neighbour whispered back, 'they've just opened for the defence.'

A famous barrister was once appearing in court on behalf of a lady with the unusual name of Tickle. He began his remarks by saying, 'Tickle, the defendant, my lord . . .'

'Tickle her yourself,' interrupted the judge. 'You're nearer than I am.'

'There are three sorts of lawyers – able, unable and lamentable.'

Robert Smith Surtees

Lawyer (to flustered witness): 'Now sir, did you or did you not, on the date in question, or at any other time, say or in any way intimate to the defendant, that the defendant was or had been in any way implicated in the events which have been described to this court, or that there was any suspicion in your mind that this may have been the case, notwithstanding that the defendant was not and could not have been in the vicinity during the period that the events aforementioned took place or might have taken place, assuming that they took place at all? Answer yes or no.'

Witness: 'Yes or no what?'

A rather unsuccessful solicitor died suddenly and his friends were very surprised when his will was disclosed because he had left very few effects.
'I suppose,' said one of his acquaintances, 'it was because he had so few causes.'

A lawyer's wife was complaining to her husband one morning at breakfast. 'We need new curtains,' she said. 'The dining room suite is a disgrace, and the whole house needs redecorating.'

'Look,' said her husband, 'I'm working on a big society divorce case at the moment. As soon as I've finished breaking up their home, I'll refurnish ours.'

Judge to defendant: 'Have you a lawyer?'
Defendant: 'No, judge, I don't need one. I'm going to tell the truth.'

A famous attorney had just won a difficult case for a lady and she approached him after the trial and said, 'How can I ever show my appreciation for what you have done?'

'Madam,' said the great lawyer, 'ever since the Phoenicians invented money, there has been only one answer to that question.'

A man accused of stealing a watch was acquitted on insufficient evidence. Outside the courtroom he approached his lawyer and said, 'What does that mean – acquitted?'

'It means,' said his lawyer, 'that the court has found you innocent. You are free to go.'

'Does that mean I can keep the watch?' asked his client.

A small town that can't support one lawyer can always support two.

A man had been convicted of theft on circumstantial evidence. When the case was sent for appeal, he revealed to his lawyer that he had been in prison at the time the crime was committed. 'Good heavens, man!' said the lawyer. 'Why on earth didn't you reveal that fact at the trial?'

'Well,' said the man, 'I thought it might prejudice the jury against me!'

Counsel: 'You are charged with stealing a motor vehicle. Have you any witnesses?'
Accused: 'No. I never take along any witnesses when I commit a robbery.'

'I wonder why it is,' said a lawyer, 'that my beard has turned grey so much sooner than my hair?'

'Because,' said a friend, 'you have worked so much harder with your jaws than with your brains.'

First man: 'And how do you earn a living?'
Second man: 'I don't. I'm a lawyer.'

Between grand theft and a legal fee, there only
stands a law degree.

A man was charged with a petty offence and the prosecuting counsel asked him, 'Can you produce anyone who can vouch for your good character?'

'Yes, sir,' said the man, 'the chief constable.' It so happened that the chief constable was in court that morning and he protested, 'Why, I don't even know the man!'

'There you are then,' said the accused. 'I have lived in this area for twenty-five years and if the chief constable doesn't know me, isn't that enough character for you?'

It is said that the reason most wives are opposed to divorce is that they don't like the idea of sharing their husband's money with a lawyer.

Lawyer: 'Excellent! You've got the most watertight case I've ever come across! The other fellow hasn't got a leg to stand on.'
Client: 'In that case, I don't think I'll pursue it any further. That was the other fellow's case I was giving you.'

Children who never come when called will grow up to be doctors.

Children who come before they are called will grow up to be lawyers.

A trial was in progress in Reykjavik, capital of Iceland, land of the midnight sun. 'Now then,' thundered counsel for the prosecution, 'Where were you on the night of December 7th to March 2nd?'

A lawyer applied to a judge for a re-trial after his client had been found guilty. 'I've uncovered important new evidence,' he said. 'What is the nature of this evidence?' asked the judge.

'Well,' said the lawyer, 'I found out this morning that my client has an extra £1000 that I didn't know about before.'

Irish barrister: 'My lord, up until now, the whole of the evidence is entirely in the dark but now the cloud of doubt begins to crack and the cat is let out of the bag!'

A prominent lawyer had overstepped the mark and was obliged to apologise to the court. He bowed to the judge and said, 'Your Honour is right and I am wrong, as your Honour generally is.' The judge is still trying to work out whether he had been complimented or insulted.

A lady asked a lawyer what was the exact difference between a solicitor and a barrister. 'Precisely the same,' replied the lawyer, 'as that between a crocodile and an alligator.'

Overbearing judge: 'Everything you say, Mr Jones, is going in at one ear and out at the other.' Smart lawyer: 'I'm sure it is, my lord. After all, what is there to stop it?'

The famous American General, Ulysses S. Grant, was a very shabby dresser and of generally unprepossessing appearance. One dark wintery night, he arrived at a small tavern in Illinois. A group of lawyers was huddled around the blazing fire. One of them noticed Grant and said jokingly, 'Here's a stranger, gentlemen, and by the looks of him, I'd say he's travelled through hell itself to get here!'

'I have indeed,' replied Grant good-humouredly. The other lawyers chuckled and the one who had spoken first said, 'And how did you find things down there?'

'Much the same as here,' replied Grant with a smile, 'lawyers all closest to the fire.'

Mark Twain once said that a jury consists of twelve persons chosen to determine which side has the better lawyer.

A notorious thief had just been acquitted on a burglary charge, thanks to the good efforts of his lawyer. Thanking the lawyer after the trial, he said, 'I'm very grateful. Perhaps I can drop in and see you some time?'

'All right,' said the lawyer, 'but make it in the daytime, will you?'

A young lawyer was visiting his club when he noticed a distinguished judge sitting by himself drinking mineral water. Thinking to ingratiate himself, he went up to the judge and said, 'Good evening, sir. Will you allow me to buy you a drink? They do a very good cocktail here made up of equal parts of brandy, rum and vodka. Have you tried it?'

'No,' grunted the judge. 'But I've tried a lot of fellows who have.'

First juror: 'We shouldn't be here very long. One look at those two fellows convinces me that they're guilty.'

Second juror: 'Not so loud, you fool! That's counsel for the prosecution and counsel for the defence!'

Judge: 'Do you have a lawyer?'

Accused: 'No.'

Judge: 'This is a serious case. Do you wish me to grant you legal aid for a lawyer?'

Accused: 'Never mind a lawyer. Just get me a couple of good witnesses.'

A very well-known lawyer was fond of displaying his knowledge of the law on any and every occasion. He was even in the habit of lecturing the office-boy on the intricacies of jurisprudence. One day, one of the office-boy's friends asked him, 'How much do they pay you at that office?' '£30,000 a year,' said the boy.

'£30,000 – for an office-boy!' said his friend, amazed.

'Yes,' said the lad. '£90 a week and the rest in legal advice.'

Prosecuting Counsel: 'Now, this man's wallet was in his inside coat pocket. He was wearing a very tight suit and it was closely buttoned. How did you manage to remove the wallet?'

Accused: 'I usually charge £250 for six lessons, sir.'

Counsel: 'Now you maintain that the man in the dock is the same man who ran into you and knocked you down with his car. Can you swear to the man?'
Witness: 'I did, but he only swore back at me and drove off.'

Counsel: 'Are you serious trying to tell the court that your husband, whom I can only in all honesty describe as a physical wreck, gave you that black eye?'

Plaintiff: 'Well, he wasn't a physical wreck until he gave me the black eye.'

It has been said that there are seven essential requisites for going to law: a good cause, a good lawyer, good evidence, good witnesses, a good judge, a good jury, and good luck!

Counsel: 'Now you say that at this point you stood up.'
Witness: 'I said I stood. How else can you stand but up?'
Counsel: 'Thank you. You may stand down.'

Solicitor: 'Are you able to pay anything at all towards the costs of the case?'

Client: 'No. I've already turned over everything I have to the judge and two of the jury.'

'A man may as well open an oyster without a knife as a lawyer's mouth without a fee.'

Barten Holyday

A farmer was engaged in litigation against his neighbour. In conversation with his lawyer, he said, 'How would it be if I sent the judge a couple of nice, fat ducks?'

'Don't you dare!' said the lawyer, aghast. 'That would completely ruin your chances.'

The case came to court and judgement was given in favour of the farmer. The lawyer was surprised and said as much to his client.

'Well, I expect it was them ducks what did it,' said the farmer with a grin.

'Good lord!' exclaimed the lawyer. 'You don't mean to say you sent them after all!'

'Yes, I did,' said the farmer, 'but I sent them in the other chap's name!'

Counsel: 'Now can you positively identify the man in the dock as the same man you saw breaking into the off-licence?'

Witness: 'Well, I think . . .'

Counsel: 'This court is not interested in what you think! We want to hear what you know!'

Witness: 'How can I tell you what I know unless I think. I can't talk without thinking – I'm not a lawyer.'

Did you hear about the very persistent young lawyer who spent a whole evening trying to break a girl's will?

Any time a lawyer is seen but not heard, it's a shame to wake him.

'Just what is a retaining fee?' a man asked a solicitor. 'Well,' said the solicitor, 'a retaining fee is the money paid to the lawyer before he will take on a case for a client.'

'Oh, I see,' said the man. 'A bit like putting money in the meter before you get any gas.'

Definition of a lawyer: a man who persuades two other men to strip for a fight and then runs off with their clothes.

A man charged with stealing a horse was acquitted after a long trial. After the trial was over, he went back to see the judge on the following day and demanded that his lawyer be arrested. 'What on earth for?' asked the judge.

'Well,' said the man, 'I didn't have enough money to pay him his fee so he went and took the horse I stole!'

An old offender listened patiently while his lawyer challenged the jurors one by one. Finally, he leaned over and whispered, 'Challenge the bloke on the bench. I've been up in front of him before and he's prejudiced against me.'

Counsel: 'Now you claim you actually saw the
defendant throw the stone?'
Witness: 'Yes.'
Counsel: 'How big was the stone?'
Witness: 'I should say it was a stone of some size.'
Counsel: 'How big exactly?'
Witness: 'Fairly large.'
Counsel: 'Can't you be more precise? Can't you
compare it with some other object?'
Witness: 'Well, I would say it was about as large as a
lump of chalk.'

'It's worth £1000 to my client,' whispered the crooked lawyer to the foreman of the jury, 'if you can manage to bring in a verdict of second degree manslaughter.'

The verdict was indeed manslaughter in the second degree and the lawyer met the juror after the trial, thanked him and paid him the money.

'It wasn't easy,' said the foreman of the jury. 'All the others wanted an acquittal.'

During a lengthy trial the judge reproved counsel for the defence for making a lot of unnecessary noise. 'I'm sorry, your Honour,' said the lawyer. 'I've lost my overcoat.'

Replied the judge, 'People often lose whole suits in here without making such a disturbance.'

'It's time you had a talk with Jimmy,' said the lawyer's wife. 'He's twelve now and there are certain things you ought to tell him – you know what I'm talking about.'

'All right, dear,' said the lawyer. 'I'll have a word with him right away.' He took his son into his study and closed the door. 'Now, Jimmy,' he said, 'it's time for us to have a man-to-man talk.'

'OK, Dad,' said Jimmy. 'What about?'

'About the alleged facts of life,' said his father.

A man consulted a lawyer about collecting a debt of £500 owed to him by a neighbour. 'Have you anything in writing to substantiate this debt?' asked the lawyer.

'No, I haven't,' said the man. 'It was a verbal agreement.'

'Then what you have to do is this,' said the lawyer. 'Write him a letter asking for immediate repayment of the £1000 he owes you.'

'But it's only £500,' protested the man.

'Exactly,' replied the lawyer. 'He'll write and tell you so and then we'll have the proof we need.'

The young lady in the witness box was a 'model' and she was revealing more and more of her assets as she crossed and recrossed her legs. Counsel for the defence suddenly jumped to his feet and said, 'Point of order, your Honour. I've just thought of something!'

'So has every other man in this courtroom,' said the judge with a smile.

In an action for damages against the owner of a dog which had worried some sheep, defence counsel claimed that it was, in fact, the plaintiff's own dog which had attacked the sheep.

'Now,' said counsel, 'you admit that the defendant's dog and your own are identical?'

'You couldn't tell the difference between them,' said the plaintiff.

'Since you were some distance away when the incident took place, how can you be so sure that it was the defendant's dog you saw and not your own?'

'Well, in the first place, my dog's been dead for three weeks . . .'

Counsel: 'What made you wait eighteen months before suing Mr Jones for calling you a hippopotamus?'

Witness: 'I didn't know what a hippopotamus looked like until I went to the zoo yesterday.'

Counsel for the defence was making his closing speech. It went on and on and on until finally the judge felt compelled to interrupt and ask that he come to a conclusion.

'I beg your pardon, my lord,' said counsel, 'but I am only acting on my client's behalf. If the verdict goes against him, he may lose his liberty for a considerable period of time. Surely I may be allowed some latitude?'

'It's not the latitude I'm complaining about,' said the judge. 'It's the longitude.'

Counsel: 'Now will you please tell the court why you didn't help the defendant in the fight?'
Witness: 'I didn't know which one was going to be the defendant, did I?'

Counsel: 'Have you followed me so far, my lord?'
Judge: 'Indeed I have, Mr Chambers, for the last hour and a half, and if I thought I could find my way back alone, I'd go back now.'

Counsel: 'Now for the last time, do you plead guilty or not guilty?'
Accused: 'How do I know until I've heard the evidence?'

Counsel: 'Now is it true that this is the fifth person you've knocked down this year?'
Accused: 'No, sir. One of them was the same person twice.'

A man was anxious to find out what profession his young son would take up so he left him in his room with a Bible, an apple and a £5 note. If he returned and found him reading the Bible, he would put him into the Church. If he was eating the apple, he would make a farmer of him. And if he was more interested in the £5 note, he would put him into finance or banking. When he finally opened the door, he found his son sitting on the Bible, eating the apple and with the £5 note in his pocket. 'That settles it!' he said. 'The boy's a born lawyer!'

A lawyer explaining to a jury the difference between presumptive and circumstantial evidence said, 'If you see a man going into a public house, that is presumptive evidence. If you see him coming out of a public house wiping his mouth, that is circumstantial evidence.'

Lawyer: 'Now where exactly did the man kiss you?'
Witness: 'On the mouth, sir.'
Lawyer: 'No, no – I mean where were you at the time!'
Witness: 'In his arms, sir.'

A burglar asked the lawyer who was defending him, 'How long do you think this business is going to last?'

'Well,' said the lawyer, 'for me about three hours. For you, I should think about three years.'

Counsel: 'Did you see the prisoner at the bar?'
Witness: 'No, sir. He was lying on his back in the street when I got to the pub.'

Irish barrister: 'Do you know what an alibi is?'
Irish defendant: 'Yes, your Honour – it's being in two places at the same time.'

A man charged with forgery protested that he couldn't even write his own name. 'Ah,' said counsel for the prosecution, 'but you're not charged with writing your own name!'

The wall between Heaven and Hell was in a poor state and badly in need of repair. St Peter asked the Devil to pay half the costs of the renovations but the Devil refused point blank to contribute a penny.

'But we have an agreement,' protested St Peter. 'If you don't pay your share, I shall sue.'

'Oh yes?' said the Devil. 'And where are you going to find a lawyer?'

Counsel: 'And just how far were you from the accident when it took place?'
Witness: 'Seventeen feet, four and a half inches.'
Counsel: 'Oh, come now! How can you be so exact?'
Witness: 'I knew some damn fool would ask me so I measured it.'

Irish barrister defending a man accused of returning a borrowed lawnmower in a damaged condition: 'My lord, I intend to prove my client's innocence in three ways. First I intend to show that he never borrowed the lawnmower in the first place. Secondly, I will show that the lawnmower was already damaged when he borrowed it. And thirdly, I will prove that it was in perfect condition when he returned it.'

Lawyer: 'If you want my honest opinion . . .'
Client: 'I don't want your honest opinion – I want your professional advice.'

A lawyer has been defined as a man who helps you get what's coming to him.

Prosecuting counsel: 'You are charged with
knocking the plaintiff down in the street and
robbing him of all his possessions except his gold
watch, a charge to which you have pleaded guilty.'
Accused: 'You mean he had a gold watch with him
at the time?'
Prosecuting counsel: 'He had.'
Accused: 'Then I'd like to change my plea to guilty
but insane.'

Counsel: 'Do you fully understand the nature of
the charge which has been brought against you?
You are accused of breaking and entering – and not
only did you take all the money you could find in
the house, you also took a large quantity of very
valuable jewellery.'
Client: 'Yes, well, my old mother used to say that
money alone does not bring happiness.'

Prosecuting counsel became fed up with the judge's continually ruling against him, and at last, he collected his papers together and began to leave the court. 'Mr Stevens,' said the judge, 'are you trying to show your contempt for this court?'

'No, your Honour,' replied the barrister. 'I am trying to conceal it.'

Counsel: 'You say that you haven't spoken to your wife for ten years? How do you explain that?'
Witness: 'I didn't like to interrupt her.'

Counsel: 'And just how far were you from the accident when it took place?'

Witness: 'Seventeen feet, four and a half inches.'

Counsel: 'Oh, come now! How can you be so exact?'

Witness: 'I knew some damn fool would ask me so I measured it.'

Irish barrister defending a man accused of returning a borrowed lawnmower in a damaged condition: 'My lord, I intend to prove my client's innocence in three ways. First I intend to show that he never borrowed the lawnmower in the first place. Secondly, I will show that the lawnmower was already damaged when he borrowed it. And thirdly, I will prove that it was in perfect condition when he returned it.'

Lawyer: 'If you want my honest opinion . . .'
Client: 'I don't want your honest opinion – I want your professional advice.'

A lawyer has been defined as a man who helps you get what's coming to him.

The wall between Heaven and Hell was in a poor state and badly in need of repair. St Peter asked the Devil to pay half the costs of the renovations but the Devil refused point blank to contribute a penny.

'But we have an agreement,' protested St Peter. 'If you don't pay your share, I shall sue.'

'Oh yes?' said the Devil. 'And where are you going to find a lawyer?'

Prosecuting counsel: 'You are charged with knocking the plaintiff down in the street and robbing him of all his possessions except his gold watch, a charge to which you have pleaded guilty.'

Accused: 'You mean he had a gold watch with him at the time?'

Prosecuting counsel: 'He had.'

Accused: 'Then I'd like to change my plea to guilty but insane.'

Counsel: 'Do you fully understand the nature of the charge which has been brought against you? You are accused of breaking and entering – and not only did you take all the money you could find in the house, you also took a large quantity of very valuable jewellery.'

Client: 'Yes, well, my old mother used to say that money alone does not bring happiness.'

A very small barrister was appearing for the defence in an important trial. Before the trial opened, he encountered counsel for the prosecution outside the courtroom. Prosecuting counsel was a giant of a man and he burst out laughing when he saw his diminutive opposite number. 'So you're my opponent, are you?' he bellowed. 'Why, I could put you in my pocket!'

'If you did,' replied the tiny barrister, 'you'd have more law in your pocket than you'll ever have in your head.'

Counsel for the defence was half-way through his summing-up when he noticed that one of the jurymen was sound asleep. 'My lord,' he said indignantly, 'I must protest! One of the jurors is asleep!'

'Well, wake him up,' said the judge. Counsel crossed to the jury box and roughly shook the man awake. 'How long have you been asleep?' he demanded.

'I don't know,' replied the juror. 'How long have you been talking?'

A young barrister got into terrible difficulties while conducting his first case and the kindly old judge intervened on several occasions. Finally, addressing opposing counsel, he said, 'I hope you don't mind, Mr Hyde-White – I am merely trying to give your young friend some ideas.'

'I shouldn't bother, my lord,' replied Mr Hyde-White, acidly. 'He's got no place to put them.'

A man who was accused of stealing a set of golf clubs was acquitted thanks to the services of a very clever lawyer. When he received his bill, he rang the lawyer and said, 'I know that £500 is quite a reasonable fee for your services but I'm afraid I can't lay my hands on that amount just at the moment. Would you settle for a brand new set of golf clubs?'

He saw a lawyer killing a viper
   On a dunghill by his own stable;
And the Devil laughed, for it put him in mind
   Of Cain, and his brother Abel.

Coleridge

Avery vain and overbearing barrister caused a great deal of amusement in court when his wig became disarranged. Unable to appreciate the joke, he appealed to the judge. 'My lord,' he said, 'do you see anything ridiculous in my wig?'

'Only your head,' replied the judge.

Counsel: 'Now do you understand the nature of an oath?'

Witness: 'I should do. I was in the car that bumped into yours at the traffic lights this morning.'

A lawyer challenged a juror who appeared in every way to be a thoroughly respectable and solid citizen. 'On what grounds is the challenge based?' asked the judge.

'On the grounds,' replied the lawyer, 'that he looks to be the sort of man who would be unduly influenced by the evidence.'

Although barristers generally show a proper respect for judges, they can at times be very scathing. One elderly counsel, on being asked by a judge on what authority he based a certain point of law, replied, 'Usher, go into the library and bring me any elementary text-book on Common Law.'

Counsel: 'Now is it true that for many years you have kept your wife under complete subjection and control?'

Witness: 'Yes, sir. I'm sorry but you see . . .'

Counsel: 'Oh, don't bother to apologise. Just tell me how you do it.'

Counsel for the defence had been on his feet for three hours and when his closing address finally ended, his opponent, a hardened old veteran, rose to his feet and said, 'My lord, I will follow the example of my learned friend and submit my case without argument.'

A man visited a lawyer in his office and asked him to act in his defence in an impending lawsuit. He outlined the facts of the case and when he had finished, the lawyer demanded an assurance that everything he had been told was the truth. 'Oh, yes,' his client replied, 'I thought it best to tell you the truth and let you put in the lies yourself.'

The judge was over half an hour late in arriving at court.

He apologised for keeping everybody waiting and explained that he had got a splinter in his finger.

A young barrister was heard to mutter to his senior, 'The old fool's been scratching his head!'

The witness was a beautiful blonde with big blue eyes. Counsel for the prosecution asked sternly, 'Now where were you on the night of Monday last?'

'I was having dinner with . . . a friend,' she replied demurely.

'And Tuesday?' counsel continued. 'I was having dinner with . . . another friend,' was the reply. Counsel leaned forward. 'And what are you doing tonight?' he murmured.

Counsel for the defence jumped to his feet. 'I object!' he cried. 'On what grounds?' said the judge. 'On the grounds that I asked her first!'

There are two kinds of lawyers: those who know the law and those who know the judge.

A very absent-minded barrister had been engaged to defend a man accused of fraud. Forgetting which side he was representing, he rose to his feet and said, 'Gentlemen of the jury, the man before you has the reputation of being one of the biggest rogues and liars in the City.'

There was a stir in the court and junior counsel tugged at his senior's sleeve and whispered urgently, 'We're appearing for the defence, sir!' Without batting an eyelid, the barrister continued, 'But what great and good man has ever lived who was not slandered by his contemporaries?'

'I don't care to speak ill of any man behind his back, gentlemen, but I believe the man who has just left the room is a solicitor.

Samuel Johnson

Lawyer, reassuring his client just before going into court: 'Now keep calm and don't lose your head. Just tell the jury, in my own words, exactly what happened.'

A claim was being made against a road haulage company for the loss of twenty-four pigs which had died in transit through negligence. 'My client has suffered a great loss,' said counsel for the plaintiff. 'This is not just a case of the loss of one or two pigs – but of twenty-four pigs! Twenty-four! Twice as many, gentlemen of the jury, as there are of you in that box!'

A man called in to see a solicitor to enlist his help in filling out a passport application. When the solicitor came to endorse the passport photograph, he absent-mindedly wrote, 'I certify that this is a true likeness of the accused.'

Counsel for the defence lost his temper with counsel for the prosecution and shouted, 'You are the biggest fool I've ever set eyes on!'

'Order, order!' said the judge sternly. 'You seem to forget that I am in the room.'

Counsel: 'Now you say you met the man at ten minutes past nine?'

Witness: 'Yes.'

Counsel: 'On a lonely country road, with no clocks about, on a dark, moonless night?'

Witness: 'Yes.'

Counsel: 'And yet you claim you remember that it was precisely ten minutes past nine! Did you speak to the man?'

Witness: 'Yes.'

Counsel: 'What did you say to him?'

Witness: I said, "Please can you tell me the time?"'

Counsel for the defence: 'You, sir, are an incompetent rogue, and before this case is over, I shall have the pleasure of showing you up for the bumbling idiot you are!'

Counsel for the prosecution: 'And you, sir, are a cheat and a liar, and know as much about the law as a child of five!'

Judge: 'Now that learned counsel have identified each other, let the case proceed.'

A young solicitor set up in practice in a small country town. For a while, business was very slow and he waited in vain for his first client. He passed the time by attending the local magistrates' court and listening to the cases; and one morning, whilst he was thus engaged, his clerk came in and whispered that there was a client waiting for him in his office. The lawyer jumped eagerly to his feet and rushed off at once. 'It's all right, sir,' his clerk shouted after him. 'He can't get away. I've locked him in.'

At a crucial point in an important criminal case, the judge adjourned so that counsel for the defence could consult with his client, whose case was going very badly, and give him the benefit of his advice as to how to proceed. Half an hour later, counsel returned but there was no sign of the accused.

'Where is the accused?' asked the judge.

'He's escaped, your Honour,' said counsel. 'That was the best advice I could give him.'

At a meeting of the bar association a famous attorney was boasting about his new glass eye. He claimed that it was so realistic that no one could tell which was the false one. All of the lawyers present nodded in astonished belief while the layman present blurted out, 'It's obvious that the left one is phoney!' The attorney, shocked that his secret was so easily discovered, asked the layman how he knew. He replied, 'Why, it's easy, the fake one is the one with a gleam of humanity.'

Irish barrister: 'Your Honour, in the case before us, I maintain that it was my client's solicitor who was at fault. From evidence which has come to light, my client was not obliged to marry the young lady at all because her father had no licence for the shotgun in the first place.'